UNTOLD
STORIES OF
advent

Mark Vincent

FAITH&LIFE
P R E S S

Newton, Kansas

Untold Stories of Advent is a collection of five stories that broaden our understanding of what God has done through the advent and birth of Jesus Christ.

Unless otherwise noted, all Scripture quotations are taken from the New Revised Standard Version, copyright @ 1990, by the Division of Christian Education of the National Council of the Churches of Christ in the United States of America, and used by permission.

Printed in the United States of America

96 95 94 93 4 3 2 1

Library of Congress Number 93-72479
International Standard Book Number 0-87303-207-1

Editorial direction for Faith & Life Press by Susan E. Janzen; copyediting by Edna Krueger Dyck; design by John Hiebert; printing by Mennonite Press, Inc. Cover art courtesy of Scala/Art Resource, NY. "Adoration of the Magi" by Domenico Ghirlandaio. Florence, Children's Hospital.

Table of Contents

Introduction

Tom Dean is my friend. He was a shoeshine boy for sixteen years, and has bagged groceries for the last three. He is single, enjoys artwork, and is an unabashed John Denver fan. Tom Dean is also a mentally challenged citizen.

Most people would not go out of their way to get to know Tom. There are many more beautiful people to befriend. Why should they strike up a relationship with Tom when relationships with mentally whole people are so much more comfortable? Getting to know Tom means getting in touch with humanity's handicaps. Most of us prefer hanging around perfection.

Those of us fortunate enough to be called Tom's friends know differently. Because we have befriended him (or because Tom has befriended us), we have been able to see past the stereotypes that surround "the retarded." Tom has taught us a fresh appreciation for God's handiwork in creation. And because we know Tom, we know a bit more of ourselves. Because I have benefited from a friendship with one of society's overlooked persons, I am beginning to see the world through God's eyes more clearly.

My purpose for this little volume is the same. The Advent season is full of precious stories—singing angels, adoring shepherds, the affectionate Madonna and child. But there are other Advent events that are not so precious to us—mysterious, ugly, troubling, bloody ones. From a distance they are not comfort producing, so they get far less attention from the Christian community than the story of Luke 2. Yet, if we study them, and if we take the time to develop a relationship with these accounts, they broaden our understanding of what God has done in the advent of Jesus Christ.

I invite you to make these stories your friends. When you have finished reading them, I think you will see the salvation of the human race as God sees it, more clearly than ever. In the story of Maher-Shalal-Hash-Baz, God uses a husband and wife committed to ministry, and the subsequent birth of their son, to change the course of history. In the birth of John the Baptist, God restores broken dreams. In the census of Caesar Augustus, God's sovereignty is demonstrated. In King Herod's consultation with Jewish religious leaders, God gives the message that mere knowledge about the first advent is not enough; those who follow Jesus need to embrace the meaning of his coming. And in the slaughter of the innocents, God brings us face-to-face with the true purpose of Advent—hope in the midst of death.

Come, make these stories your friends.

Mark Vincent

THE SIGN OF THE MESSIAH

herefore the Lord himself will give you a sign. Look, the young woman is with child and shall bear a son, and shall name him Immanuel. He shall eat curds and honey by the time he knows how to refuse the evil and choose the good. For before the child knows how to refuse the evil and choose the good, the land before whose two kings you are in dread will be deserted. The LORD will bring on you and on your people and on your ancestral house such days as have not come since the day that Ephraim departed from Judah — the king of Assyria.

Isaiah 7: 14-17

And I went to the prophetess, and she conceived and bore a son. Then the LORD said to me, Name him Maher-Shalal-Hash-Baz; for before the child knows how to call "My father" or "My mother," the wealth of Damascus and the spoil of Samaria will be carried away by the king of Assyria.

Isaiah 8: 3-4

It was a wicked time. A wicked king sat on the throne. This king sacrificed to many gods and killed several of his children in sacrifice. He may have fathered his first child at the age of eleven. He led his people into corrupt activity and transgression.

It was a difficult time. The kingdom was embattled. Armies from two northern kingdoms had invaded the land. Although the wicked king was not defeated, his army suffered heavy losses. Many of his people had been carried off as slaves; many more had experienced the ravages of war. To make matters worse, a southern kingdom had raided outlying areas while the king was protecting his land from the northern invaders.

It was a dangerous time. In a last ditch effort, the king sent what treasures remained to a far-eastern empire, hoping they would accept the treasures as payment to come, and would defeat the northern enemies—but there were no guarantees.

It was a treacherous time. The wicked king began sacrificing to his enemy's gods because they seemed more powerful. The land plunged into despair because no one knew if the empire would come to the rescue. If they did, could they be trusted? Would they defeat just the armies of the North or would greed lead the empire to plunder their kingdom as well?

It was a fearful time. The wicked king consulted with a prophet. What would the outcome be? The prophet sought his God and was given a sign—the birth of a child—but not just any birth and not just any child. This child would be born to a virgin, a biologically impossible feat. The child would be named "God with us." Before this god-child left the stage of innocence, the empire would come and defeat the northern enemies. But there was more. Yes, the enemies would be defeated, but the country over which the wicked king ruled would become a place of devastation.

It was a time of disbelief. How could the people believe a sign they could not see? How could they believe in a god-child when his coming seemed so far away? They needed a sign right now in order to understand God's intentions. So the prophet took a tablet and in large letters wrote the words, "Spoil Quickly, Plunder Speedily," and hung it for all to see. A priest and an elder statesman were called in to bear witness to what was written.

Then the prophet went home to his wife, a prophetess, and embraced her. They united in intercourse and she conceived her second child. At the proper time a son was born and God spoke again to the prophet, telling him to name his son with the title written on the sign: "Spoil Quickly, Plunder Speedily." The wicked king was informed the child was the immediate sign he had wished for, and that before this babe was old enough to identify his parents in speech, the eastern empire would arrive and defeat the invading northern armies. But again there was more. The empire and its enormous army would be like a swollen river which has spilled its banks with nothing to check it. Yes, the northern oppressors would be swept away, drowned beneath the advance of the empire, but the wicked king and his land would be neck deep in the flood waters. Would they be destroyed like the lands to the north? No, but their suffering would be worse than anything the northern armies had done to them.

It was a time of hope. Even in the neck-deep floodwaters of the eastern empire, even in the destruction that was to come, the god-child's birth came ever nearer. The invading armies might sweep over the land, but they could not permanently defeat it. This place would be the land of the virgin-born god-child, "God with us." No matter how fierce or murderous the battle cry of invading nations, no matter the distance the armies had traveled, no matter how thorough the preparations for battle, no matter how cunning the strategy, no matter how brilliant the plans: no army would stand against "God with us." Upon his coming, the armies would find their plans thwarted and their most sophisticated weaponry shattered. The god-child would be the victor.

It was a time to decide one's faith. Could the wicked king believe the words of the prophet he had consulted?

Could the people bring themselves to do the unnatural thing and cease protecting their homeland? Could the kingdom accept God's verdict of punishment and ultimate hope? Could they believe the birth of the prophet's son, "Spoil Quickly, Plunder Speedily," was proof enough that the god-child would also be born? Could they accept God's working in history? Could they grasp and believe in God's purposes? Could they let God do the fighting for them? Only time would tell. The prophet had decided though. His faith was placed in God's plan. It would not be easy. The way would be hard. Those who lived near him would taunt him and accuse him of collaborating with the eastern empire to insure the kingdom's defeat. But this prophet had a sense of purpose. After all hadn't God miraculously given a son as a sign of the divine plan? How could the prophet do anything else but believe?

This is the story of Isaiah. The events can be found in 2 Kings 16, 2 Chronicles 28, and Isaiah 7—8. The wicked king is King Ahaz. His kingdom is Judah. Israel and Syria are the northern invaders. The eastern empire he called upon for assistance is Assyria. The virgin would appear 700 years later as the young girl Mary. Her son named "God with us" (Immanuel) would be the Christchild. The prophetess was Isaiah's wife and the son named "Spoil Quickly, Plunder Speedily" was their son Maher-Shalal-Hash-Baz.

There is much to learn here about God's working in his-

tory. There is beauty here which one finds in trying to understand the purposes of the coming Christ, but my interest is
piqued by the family at the center of all this. When one works
one's way through the prophecies about the coming god-
child, and gets to the bottom of all the armies and political
maneuverings, there is a family of four—Isaiah, his prophetess wife, and two sons. What lessons can we learn from them?
What principles can be grasped in the birth and naming of
their son who was the sign of God's intentions? I find at least
three answers to such questions—the individual, community,
and spiritual importance of this specially named child.

A Name Communicates Individual Importance

The naming of any child is important. It communicates that
this unique person was a special act of God's creation and is
unlike any other created being. Names are given to children
so individual distinctions can be made. The name helps the
child maintain a sense of individuality. Isaiah's son certainly
would come to learn his uniqueness and importance. With a
name like Maher-Shalal-Hash-Baz, any child would know he
is different from others. How do you call a child like this in
from outside, anyway? What kind of nickname do you give
him? Shalaz? Mahash? Shazam?

As this son matured, he would come to understand that
his special name spoke of his uniqueness, of a special God-

inspired calling for his life. Whenever his name was spoken, it would remind all who heard it of God's punishment of a wicked king and his people, and the promise of the future god-child.

My name, Mark, means warrior or defender. It is derived from Mars, the warrior god of Greek mythology. Granted, it may not be much of a name for a pacifist, but early in life my parents taught me the importance of this name. They knew God wanted to do something unique through me; God had gifted me like no other person to accomplish kingdom work in the world. They wanted me to become God's warrior—a guardian of the Christian faith. I do not hear my name without being reminded of my individual importance.

My daughter's name, Autumn, speaks of the harvest beauty we see each year—the golds, reds, and browns, the drying corn, and the abundance of crops that are brought in from the fields. It may not be a familiar name, but Lorie and I wish to teach her its importance. We want her to know that God has created a beauty within her and mixed together a combination of physical characteristics given to no other human. We want her to know God's intention for her to find beauty in the world and to share it with others. We want the very sound of her name to remind her of her importance and value as an individual.

Our son's name, Zachary, comes from the biblical name Zechariah, which means "Yahweh remembers." Lorie and I wish to teach him the importance of such a name. We want him to open God's Word and find a special kinship with the prophet whose name he bears. We want him to know we believe Yahweh remembered us in giving him to our family. We want him to know Yahweh will never forget him. We want the very sound of his name to be a reminder of how important and valued he is.

Children are specific acts of God's creation. They bear the detailed marks of divine design. God invests in each child, giving to each child a unique combination of gifts to do a special work that changes the face of history. Have they been told this? Are they daily told how important their parents and God think they are? A child's name is an important thing. The sound of it communicates individual importance and significance.

A Name Communicates Community Importance

The meaning of Maher-Shalal-Hash-Baz, "Spoil Quickly, Plunder Speedily," carried community importance. The surrounding nations experienced destruction because of this child. His name was a reminder that the land in which he lived had been overrun by the eastern Assyrian empire. His name was a permanent residue of God's judgment. His name was a beacon of the people's coming hope, the god-child Immanuel. Maher-Shalal-Hash-Baz grew up knowing his importance to the community.

My parents often told me I had a special role in my community. Even now, when they visit, they are sure to say, "Mark, you are special. God is doing things through you. You are making a difference. We couldn't be more proud." Each time I am near them, I come away filled with a sense of worth, a knowledge I can give hope to the world around me.

Autumn already contributes to the community. Her presence in any room is an attention getter. Her love for music and her dancing response to it has warmed many hearts in her six years. Our responsibility as parents is to help her realize the important role she plays in the world around her—to help her spread God's beauty so a beautiful harvest is gathered for the kingdom.

Zachary and his personality are just becoming known to us. He is so young, but he already plays an important role. Already, many adults have looked at our son and remarked on the beauty of God's creation. When he was just an infant he was already teaching people that Yahweh remembers, and he had yet to utter a word. Lorie and I must help him understand how he did this. We must show him that because of his importance to his community, he must find some way to tell his world, "Yahweh remembers."

Parents can find another lesson here. For children to find fulfillment as adults they must come to appreciate the give and take of community, and the importance of participation in that community. They should be told this often—the community needs a person like them, uniquely put together by God at this time in history to play a role no one else can play. More than this, they need to see the nurturing adults around them demonstrating what healthy community looks like.

A Name Communicates Spiritual Importance

The source of the name, Maher-Shalal-Hash-Baz, is in two places—God and the parents. Yes, God dictated the name. Yes, God is the One who determined the special role the child would play for the nation of Judah. But, the parents consented. Mom and Dad listened to God. As this boy grew, he would often hear the story of his birth and of God's involvement in the circumstances. He would also hear stories of his parents' faith and of their decision to give service to God. His growing up would be difficult—being a boy with God-serving parents in an idolatrous world. With his unique name and a birth that pointed to the coming Immanuel and God's message to let Immanuel do the fighting, his childhood would be hard. Many who surrounded him would taunt him. Many days he would wish his name had been given to some-one else, and that service to God would not demand so much.

But in the end, by God's grace, his spiritual heritage and his parents' love would bring him to see that service to God far outweighs the pressures of a pagan environment.

My name and my childhood experiences grow out of several generations of Christian faith. The stories of my grandparents and their obedience to God are precious to me. The witness of my parents and their desire to discuss faith issues runs strong in my blood. I did not always appreciate this. I was not always sure I wanted to be different from the surrounding world in this way. But in the end the spiritual source of my name won out, and my desire became and still is to give unyielding service to God.

The children in our home, Autumn and Zachary, are surrounded by spiritual things. We do not want our spirituality to be some sticky goo, liberally applied with trite answers and chintzy prayers. Rather, we wish it to be a fine frosting, bringing sweetness and comfort to life. Selecting names for our children took careful discernment. Not only did we want them to understand their worth as individuals and their importance to the community, we wanted them to know how much we valued our faith and how much we hope they will choose to share in it. Their life won't always be easy. Swimming upriver against a stream of humanity that denies the value of spiritual things is a difficult prospect. There will be days they wish God hadn't placed them in our family, days they wish they could disappear into the background and remain incognito. With God's help, the faith stories of grandparents and parents will work the desired effect and our children will embrace our God as theirs. Our hope is that they will believe in Immanuel, the God-child born on a star-filled night in Bethlehem, the promised one who gives a reason to cease fighting with others.

Perhaps if more parents could learn this story of a son born to be a sign for a troubled nation—or hear more descriptions of parents who teach children their importance to the community—then maybe more parents would respond. Children do not need to hear how inconvenient they are to the parents' lifestyle. They do not need to be treated as nuisances. They need to be told of their worth, of their uniqueness and of the special work God wants to do through them. Most of all, they must be told again and again the stories of their parents' faith.

I am creating a name for my children. Will they look at it as a holy destiny or as a twisted act of fate?

THE BIRTH OF JOHN THE BAPTIST

ow the time came for Elizabeth to give birth, and she bore a son. **H**er neighbors and relatives heard that the Lord had shown his great mercy to her, and they rejoiced with her. **O**n the eighth day they came to circumcise the child, and they were going to name him Zechariah after his father. **B**ut his mother said, "No, he is to be called John." **T**hey said to her, "None of your relatives has this name." **T**hen they began motioning to his father to find out what name he wanted to give him. **H**e asked for a writing tablet and wrote, "His name is John." **A**nd all of them were amazed. **I**mmediately his mouth was opened and his tongue freed, and he began to speak, praising God.

Luke 1:57-64

Do you have dreams that no longer seem attainable? Someday I would like to live in a remote cabin framed by water and Douglas fir, filled with the smells of fresh pine and baking bread, and the sound of wood crackling in one of several fireplaces. Yet, with the escalation of real estate prices, the investments I have chosen instead and the fact I live in a housing addition, this dream has become a wistful "wouldn't it be nice," instead of something I am actively pursuing.

Some of you have dreams like this. Perhaps you dream of owning the ultimate driving machine, or taking an exotic vacation in Tahiti, or becoming independently wealthy so you can quit your job. We all know these dreams are quite unlikely to happen due to our life circumstances.

Others have broken dreams. You wish your family could live together in peace. Or you hope for a financial windfall, so outstanding medical bills could be covered. Or you are hoping for something more than temporary employment. But the wind seems to be blowing against you—the likelihood of these things happening is fading quickly.

Such was the case with Elizabeth and Zechariah, a couple faithfully following God as spiritual leaders in the midst of religious and political corruption. The one thing they hoped for—a child—was no longer possible for them. Zechariah was a priest and Elizabeth was the daughter of a priest. Their lives had been spent in religious service for the nation of Israel. They lived in a world in which a woman's worth was measured by her ability to bear children. They lived in a world where a man's prosperity corresponded to the number of sons he fathered. They lived in a world that viewed eternal life not so much as life in heaven, but in keeping the covenant God made with Abraham in each succeeding generation. Yet, after years of anticipation, they remained childless. Zechariah and Elizabeth were now in their twilight years, beyond physiological ability to bear children. Their dream to have a child had become a regret.

The twenty thousand priests of Zechariah's day were divided into twenty-four groups, each group numbering over eight hundred priests. Each group was on duty for one week every six months. The group to which Zechariah belonged was eighth out of the twenty-four groups and happened to be on duty when Zechariah received his vision.

During the week of temple service, priests drew lots for the various responsibilities associated with the morning and evening sacrifices. One of the most special duties was offering incense from the golden altar. The priest who did this waited until the assembled worshipers exited to the temple courtyard and knelt in worship. Then, alone, he would enter the holy place of the temple, spread the coals across the golden altar, and light them. In that moment the actions of the priest symbolized the prayers of a nation lifted to God. Priests seldom offered incense more than once in their lifetime because there were so many priests. Should a priest be fortunate to offer incense during his week of service, his name was taken out of the pool for which the lot was cast. On this particular day it was Zechariah's turn.

Perhaps the angel was inside the temple waiting for him. Perhaps the angel waited until the offering of incense was complete before making himself known. In any case, encountering the angel certainly surprised the aging priest. Luke tells us that Zechariah was "gripped with fear" (1:12 NIV). The angel then spoke saying, "Do not be afraid, Zechariah; for your prayer has been heard. Your wife Elizabeth will bear you a son, and you are to give him the name John" (1:13). Had Zechariah been praying for such a miracle, perhaps even as he had entered the holy place to offer the incense? Was this a prayer he had prayed in their childbearing years and had since given up? Or was it that Zechariah had been faithfully praying for the Messiah, and God's way of rewarding his prayers was not only to tell him Messiah was coming (Luke 1:17), but to give him the child he had longed for? We cannot know the answer to these questions—but we can know Zechariah had been praying, and he prayed to a God who heard his prayers.

A Child of Preparation

The angel continued the announcement by telling the father-to-be more information about the impending birth. Clearly this would be no normal baby, but a child of preparation.

The angel told Zechariah his son would be a joy and delight to more than his parents, but also to the nation of Israel. In order to accomplish this God would give the child an incredible gift. He would be filled with the Holy Spirit from birth. This gift would enable him to minister in the power and spirit of Elijah the prophet. In addition, this son would prepare for his ministry by becoming a Nazirite—one who abstained from certain activities in order to show he was set apart for the service of God. In this way, we see both divine and human elements involved in the preparation. God would empower the baby for a ministry. The parents and the child were to be sure he obeyed his Nazirite responsibilities and was ready when the ministry began.

Once the individual preparations for John's ministry were completed, his ministry would become one of preparing Israel for the Messiah. According to the angel's announcement, John would prepare Israel in four ways.

First, there would be repentance. The angel said, "He will turn many of the people of Israel to the Lord their God" (Luke 1:16). Evidently, a result of John's ministry would be lapsed Jews returning to their synagogues and temple worship, renewing their covenant with God and observing God's commandments once again.

Second, Israel would experience renewed family life. The angel's words were, "With the spirit and power of Elijah he will go before him, to turn the hearts of parents to their children" (Luke 1:17). Nothing specifically wrong with Israel's homes is mentioned here, but there was an apparent need for family life to be strengthened. We do know of one ongoing problem the Jewish family faced. Because of their sin before God the Jews had been scattered throughout the Roman Empire, taking their culture and religion with them. Now, however, the Greek language and culture which pervaded the empire threatened Jewish distinctives. Many Jewish children could not speak Hebrew, some no longer circumcised their offspring, even more disregarded fine points of the Mosaic Law. I find it easy to conceive that this cultural tension produced a rift between older and younger generations—especially among fathers and sons, who functioned as the heads of their respective Jewish homes. If this is true, John's ministry would help find healing for homes divided over fundamental religious issues.

Third, Israel would see a renewed righteousness. Because of John's ministry, people previously disobedient through rejecting the word of God would now turn and embrace righteousness. In other words, John's ministry would result in spiritual conversion.

Fourth, John would be responsible for making ready a people prepared for the Lord. John would do more than broadcast the announcement of Jesus Messiah and his ministry. He would prepare a people who would form the core of Jesus' followers and ultimately the Christian church.

The angel's announcement and explanation was now finished. Poor Zechariah was overwhelmed by all this. So much had happened in one day. A rare opportunity to light incense during a worship service, the appearance of an angel, and now the information the angel had given. He was going to be a father! This went beyond the realm of possibility! "How can I be sure what you are telling me is true?" Zechariah wanted to know. "We are old people!"

The angel's reply is extremely direct. "You can be sure of this because I am Gabriel. I stand in the presence of God. I am God's messenger of good news to you. If you want a sign then here it is. You will be unable to speak until the day your son is born. You will be struck mute because you did not believe my words were true—and they are."

Evidently the dialogue between these two broke off at this point. At least no further conversation is recorded for us. Meanwhile, the assembled congregation was waiting for Zechariah to come out. They were getting cramps and muscle aches from kneeling so long. Normally, lighting the incense was a simple process. Was the old priest having difficulty getting the incense lit? Worse yet, had he suffered a stroke or heart attack? Their questions were answered when Zechariah appeared, unable to speak. Somehow through his gestures, they perceived Zechariah had encountered a vision while ministering inside the temple walls.

Apparently, a couple of days of temple service remained for Zechariah's group of priests, and Zechariah finished them even though he could not speak. Verse 23 tells us that once his priestly duties were completed, Zechariah returned to his home in the hill country of Judea. This verse is absolutely necessary for the remainder of the story! Had Zechariah not returned home and acted upon his vision, Elizabeth would not have become pregnant! I smile when I imagine what it was like for them. Zechariah, who could no longer speak, trying to communicate the angel's message to Elizabeth, who probably could not read. Perhaps an educated servant or a relative read to Elizabeth what Zechariah wrote about his experience inside the temple. I would guess it was an occasion for sheepishness, giggling, and renewed amorousness between this godly couple.

Soon, this child who was to prepare Israel for the Messiah was on his way. Elizabeth actually became pregnant! This child destined to prepare a people for the Messiah was coming. The promise of the angel was true.

A Child of Promise

Elizabeth went into seclusion upon finding out she was pregnant—partly because of custom and partly, I'm sure, because it was awkward for a graduate of menopause to explain why she had morning sickness. During this time Elizabeth celebrated the forthcoming birth of her promised son. "This is what the Lord has done for me," she said. "He looked favorably on me and took away my disgrace I have endured among my people" (Luke 1:25). She says this because her barrenness, coupled with an apparently righteous life, may have led some to conclude secret sin of Elizabeth's past had contributed to her inability to have children. Thus, being pregnant, she celebrates her vindication. I am certain John's role in God's plan was important to her, but her celebration is in the promise of his life—a reward for her faithful service to God—an opportunity to actually be a mother and share the experience of other women.

So much of Scripture is filled with women looking forward to the birth of promised children: Sarah laughing at the prospect she might have a son, yet becoming pregnant. Rebekah remaining barren for many years, then having twins. Rachel, sorrowful that Leah has many children and she has none, yet eventually giving birth to a son who would rescue Egypt from famine. Hannah weeping at the tabernacle because she could have no children, but cradling a son in her arms a year later. The wife of Manoah, receiving the promise of an angel that she would have a son — a son named Samson — who would rescue Israel. Neither should we forget Isaiah, his wife, and all Israel looking forward to the sign which meant Israel would be rescued from its oppressors—the birth of Maher-Shalal-Hash-Baz. Now we have Zechariah and Elizabeth expecting as well. Each of these children serves as a child of promise, pointing the way to the ultimate child of promise, Jesus Christ, whose birth we celebrate each Christmas.

A Child of Praise

At this point Luke's narrative about Elizabeth and Zechariah breaks off into another strand. Elizabeth's younger relative, Mary, receives the announcement that she will bear the Messiah. The story of John's birth picks up again in verse 39, when upon hearing Gabriel's announcement, Mary hurries to visit Elizabeth. During the visit between these two women we discover John is also a child of praise.

I liken the joy Elizabeth and Mary had upon seeing each other to the joy between my wife and her sister when they discovered they would both be mothers. Such laughter has not been heard in my house before or since. I have never seen a phone bill so high either! They were like little kids in their joyful celebration of motherhood. I think this is the source of Elizabeth's and Mary's joy. Two soon-to-be moms, both carrying miracle babies—babies upon which rest God's plans for the human race. When they met, how could they keep from praising the One who made all this possible?

First to offer praise is Elizabeth, saying to Mary in a loud, Spirit-filled voice, "Blessed are you among women, and blessed is the child you will bear! But why am I so favored, that the mother of my Lord should come to me? As soon as the sound of your greeting reached my ears, the baby in my womb leaped for joy. Blessed is she who has believed that what the Lord has said to her will be accomplished!" (Luke 1:42-45 NIV). Obviously, Elizabeth senses the immensity of God's work within those two wombs. She goes so far as to call Mary's child her Lord. Elizabeth already recognizes this child as the long-awaited Messiah!

Then Mary praises God, offering up a song we call the Magnificat, one of the most loved songs found in Scripture. As we look at the meeting of these two women, we see an atmosphere of praise, of extreme joy being expressed to the God who made it possible.

We are told that Mary stayed with Elizabeth for three months, nearly to the end of Elizabeth's pregnancy. When Elizabeth gave birth, Luke tells us matter-of-factly, the child was a son. This was a cause of celebration for neighbors and relatives as well as the new parents. Not only did God allow Elizabeth to give birth in old age, but Zechariah had a son, which meant God's covenant with Abraham continued on for another generation within Zechariah's family. Eight days later came the circumcision. Tradition said a firstborn son received his father's name. In fact, everyone was already calling this boy Zechariah out of habit. Thus Elizabeth startled everyone when she said this boy's name was to be John. Not even a relative had this name! Surely this broke with tradition! But then, so did having children at such an advanced age.

Those gathered for the circumcision ceremony turned to the mute father and asked him what the child's name should be. He motioned for a tablet and wrote a simple sentence, "His name is John." Immediately, Zechariah's tongue was loosed and a flood of praise to God poured forth. Many think the first words Zechariah uttered were those of his praise song, the Benedictus, which is recorded in the following verses, a song he had spent nine months preparing. Surely we can see this child was a source of praise to God.

A Child of Ponderings

Now, consider the crowd of friends and relatives who had witnessed all these events. They knew and loved this old couple. They knew Zechariah had received a vision. They knew he could not speak. They knew Elizabeth had conceived and birthed a child when she was beyond the natural ability to do so. They heard them give this child an unexpected name. They witnessed the miracle of a mute man suddenly speaking.

What do you think your response would have been at the birth of this child and the surrounding events had you been present? I think you might have been reduced to thoughtful reflection. Luke writes, "The neighbors were all filled with awe, and throughout the hill country of Judea people were talking about all these things. Everyone who heard this wondered about it, asking, 'What then is this child going to be?' For the Lord's hand was with him" (Luke 1:65,66 NIV).

This was a child of ponderings. His birth left everyone wondering about the meaning of these events and the purpose of this child's life. Surely God's hand was on him from the start, just as Gabriel had promised Zechariah in the vision.

It is wise for us to ask the same questions. What does the birth of John the Baptist mean? His birth makes an enchanting story, but should it make any difference to me?

The answer to both questions is certain. John's birth forecast the coming of the Messiah, and the Messiah is of great meaning to Christians. The Messiah is both Savior and the object of our worship. Hearing the story of John's birth should mean we consider anew how God prepared the chosen people. Hearing Zechariah's vision should lead us to contemplate the promises of God to the chosen people, as well as to individual believers. Just as God promised the coming of the Messiah and the birth of John to a couple who were both Jewish and childless, so you must think about God's promises to you as the chosen people and to you as an individual. Thinking about Zechariah, Elizabeth, and their young relative Mary should also lead you toward praise. God works miracles! Nothing is impossible for God! God can make the barren fruitful. God can cause the virgin to give birth. God can restore the hopes of a nation through the birth of a child. Certainly God is deserving of praise. Hearing this story should cause us to ponder the meaning of these events, just as we have been doing.

As I pondered the meaning of these events I discovered God isn't only concerned with the course of human history, but with the individual dreams of the men and women God created. God especially honors those who have set aside their selfish dreams for God's plans. This is the example of Zechariah and Elizabeth, a couple not embittered with a God who left them barren, but committed to faithful service. This is the example of the faithful community of Israel awaiting the long expected Messiah even though it seemed God had abandoned them.

This does not mean God will give me the log cabin I want just because I am obedient. It does not mean your family burdens will suddenly lift themselves either, or that your financial woes will suddenly cease. It does mean that sincere obedience to God is more important than your dreams—

whether or not they come true. It also means God will not forget about us. God uses obedient people with their broken dreams. God accomplishes something in them far greater than they ever would have wished for. This is what this often over-looked Christmas event means. When we make God's dream of salvation our own, the broken dreams we leave behind either no longer matter — or are gloriously fulfilled.

the Census

n those days a decree went out from Emperor Augustus that all the world should be registered. This was the first registration and was taken while Quirinius was governor of Syria. All went to their own towns to be registered. Joseph also went from the town of Nazareth in Galilee to Judea, to the city of David called Bethlehem, because he was descended from the house and family of David. He went to be registered with Mary, to whom he was engaged and who was expecting a child. While they were there, the time came for her to deliver her child. And she gave birth to her firstborn son and wrapped him in bands of cloth, and laid him in a manger, because there was no place for them in the inn.

Luke 2:1-7

The servant of a wealthy man was making purchases in the marketplace when he ran into Death. That's right. Death. The fellow with the black hood that covers his skull-like face, and who carries that antique farm implement.

The servant was surprised to see Death out in public, but he was even more surprised when Death apparently made threatening gestures towards him. The servant fled to the home of his master and requested that he be allowed to travel to Samarra. When the master asked why, the servant said, "I encountered Death at the marketplace a few moments ago, and apparently he has come for me. If I leave now I can be in Samarra by nightfall. I will lie low for a few days and then return. Perhaps I can escape my fate."

The master gave his permission. So the servant finished his hurried packing and made his departure. Later that day the master made his way to the marketplace where he too found Death. "Death," the master said, "why did you threaten my servant so?" Death replied, "I did not threaten your servant; it was an expression of surprise. I wasn't expecting to see him here for I have an appointment with him in Samarra tonight."

This is a rather morbid story, one that shows us that many of life's events are out of our control in spite of what we do to avoid them. It was the servant's time to die. Even with his efforts to the contrary, death would overtake him. I have seen a similar pattern in my own life with things I said I would never do but ended up doing. I was never going to attend the local Bible college—everyone I knew attended there! Guess where my degree came from! I had no desire to date the dark-haired beauty who cleaned my dad's office, especially because my dad had recommended her. Guess who proposed to her less than a year later! I was never going to live in Fort Wayne, especially on the near northwest side of downtown, a neighborhood that gave this suburban boy the heebie-jeebies. Guess which zip code I had for nine years! I was never going to be a pastor. An itinerant preacher maybe, but never a pastor. Guess which profession puts food on my table!

All of these things formed my druthers, but I have honored none of them. Why? Because although I felt strongly about these things, I felt even more strongly about faithfully serving my Lord, and God has clearly led me down this path. In doing so God used events—like my father taking a job at the college I didn't want to attend, thus making it extremely affordable—to help me view matters differently. God used events like my best friend dating a good friend of my dad's cleaning lady. The cleaning lady and I would often tag along. When our friends stopped dating, we started. And that, as they say, was that. God used events like a much needed part-time job as a youth pastor to bring me to the inner-city church where I later became the pastor. In spite of my wishes.

In spite of the plans I had set for myself. Even in spite of the choices I had made. God has worked in the midst of them, even using the choices of others to influence my own.

Other people could tell similar tales. Some have come from farming communities to the city—a choice they would not have made on their own. Somehow God worked through the military draft, and their conscientious objection to it, to bring them there. Others can point to the working of God in their life in spite of immoral choices they made. Somehow God worked within these choices to turn them back. They could not have discovered a relationship with God by themselves, no matter how valiant their attempt, yet God brought them in.

Some could point to the working of God in spite of injustice. Even though life has not treated them fairly, God has used unjust circumstances to fashion maturity in them and to show them that God's plan is being worked out regardless. Were each of them to tell their story, we would hear numerous examples of God working within bizarre, unexpected circumstances to accomplish God's perfect will.

I think Caesar Augustus would corroborate what I have just written. God used Caesar Augustus in a way he never would have expected—to bring about the salvation of the human race. Augustus knew little or nothing about Jehovah. He had become a priest for the Roman religion at the tender age of sixteen and had worshiped the Roman gods through-out his life. He was also an immoral man, making a habit of deflowering the virgins Livia, his wife, would find for him. He ordered the murder of at least one potential rival when he gained control of the Roman Empire. He banished family members from Rome for violating the public code of morality he expected of Roman citizens but never followed himself. Yet this ungodly man was used to accomplish God's purposes.

Caesar Augustus is credited with establishing the Roman Empire and for creating a form of government that lasted nearly five hundred years. Historians believe this sickly little man with bad teeth, pitted skin, and piercing gaze "was one of the most talented, energetic and skillful administrators this world has ever known" (Michael Grant, *The Roman Emperors: A Biographical Guide to the Rulers of Imperial Rome,* New York: Charles Scribner's Sons, 1985, p.15).

If any ruler was concerned with posterity, Caesar Augustus was. He was a great orator and prolific writer, mak-ing notes for everything he said, including conversations with his wife. He took great pains to be sure records of his rule were extremely accurate. He placed tremendous efforts in ensuring the success of the one who would inherit his throne. He even wore elevator shoes so he would appear taller. He wanted to be remembered as the one who improved Rome's commerce, as the one who encouraged intellectual pursuits, as the one who improved travel, trade, and the local economy. Yet, God used a decision so insignificant that Augustus's historians didn't bother to record it to fulfill the prophecy of the Christchild being born in Bethlehem. As a result, Caesar Augustus is more famous for his census than for anything else he did.

When we consider Caesar Augustus's census, we see God using the most obscure of circumstances to bring about salvation for the human race. If we reflect on what this means, we discover a reason to have a hope in the future, regardless of the events we face. If God could use a decision made in Italy to bring the Christchild to Bethlehem, hundreds of miles away, God can certainly use the most peculiar event in history to bring about the kingdom. God can also use any event we face to further work in us.

The Right Authority

Let's look further at this obscure census and see how it was for God's own purposes. First, we discover the right kind of authority was involved.

The census Augustus ordered covered what was called the inhabited world, a term the Romans borrowed from the Greeks to describe the Roman Empire. Apparently it was the first of two such censuses Augustus ordered. The second one occurred eleven years later and is referred to in Acts 5:37. We are unsure whether this census was to merely number the population or to be a tool for forming a tax roll. But we do know that only a king with the authority of Caesar Augustus could have carried it out. The Roman Peace (Pax Romana) had begun under his rule. This was a two-hundred-year period in which the empire, with the exception of regional uprisings, enjoyed a cessation of warfare. An emperor powerful enough to enjoy a time of peace could turn his attention away from military matters and focus on administrative concerns, like ordering a census.

Not only did Augustus have the authority to order such a census, he had astute regents beneath him who served him well. One of those was King Herod, tetrarch of Judea. Herod apparently held up the census for a couple of years, perhaps for administrative reasons, but once he carried it out he did so in a politically sensitive way. Herod, like Augustus, was a government leader concerned with self-preservation. Yet, it seems God worked within Herod's selfishness so that Herod formed a consensus administration policy Jews could support. When Jews registered, they were to return to their tribal homelands and register in the cities of their ancestors. Although Herod may have done this for selfish reasons, it allowed the Jews to feel their traditions were valued by the government which ruled over them, and it secured their cooperation.

This census policy is what took Mary and Joseph—both of whom were descendants of the house of David, and both probably Benjaminites now living in the north—back to the original city of David, Bethlehem. Augustus could not have known this, neither could Herod—at least not until the Wise Men came. Yet, God used this to fulfill the prophecy of Micah 5:2: "But you O Bethlehem of Ephrathah, who are one of the little clans of Judah, from you shall come forth for me one who is to rule in Israel."

There is one other authority present in this story, one we must not overlook. It is the authority God has in the declarations of the Word. God is the only one in the universe powerful enough to declare what will happen centuries ahead of time and who lives long enough and is authoritative enough to bring those declarations to fruition. And this is what God does. God's authority is behind the entire Christmas event, from the promise of Gabriel to Mary, to the star placed in the heavens, to the song of the angels, to the census which Augustus ordered a couple of years before the Christchild was born. If God's authority overarches the authority of the world's greatest emperors, then God's authority is capable of working within current events of human history to bring about the kingdom.

I believe God is still in the business of using the right authority, and will do so to bring about the second coming of

Christ. We read the news and worry about what troublesome world leaders will do next. We pray, asking God to influence our government leaders away from addiction to power. We wince when we hear of the latest violent confrontation in our world. Yet, in the midst of the most corrupt government God has placed the right authority. The men and women who rule this world, no matter how noble or decadent, are there for a purpose. God is using them to prepare this world for Christ's return.

The same can be said about the minor authorities that exist in your life. Whether kind or overbearing, God can work through them to teach you and to prepare you for further ministry. If we really believe God was capable of working through the authority of Caesar Augustus to bring the babe to Bethlehem, then we can believe God is certainly capable of working within your circumstances.

The Right Timing

Another observation about the census is that it took place at the right time. The Roman period of peace was unprecedented in human history. Never before had the world seen such prosperity. Never before were people able to engage in international travel in such safety. Never before had an international governmental structure of this magnitude succeeded for this long. All others had been overthrown or reduced to internal chaos. This period not only provided an occasion for the birth of the Christchild so it would fulfill Old Testament prophecies, but also made possible the rapid spread of Christianity. This is certainly not what was intended by the Roman Empire. But God used the timing of these events for a divine purpose.

The census decree and the way it was administered were also timely. Think about this. A census decree is delivered in approximately 8 B.C.E. The local regent delays carrying it out for a couple of years for political reasons, and when he does so it coincides with the final days of Mary's pregnancy.

This decree also comes during the height of Jewish expectations for the Messiah. People like Zechariah, Elizabeth, Simeon, and Anna had spent their entire lives praying and waiting for the advent of their Lord. Every generation someone arose who purported to be the Messiah, and thousands of Jews would follow with the expectation that God was now ready to establish the kingdom (Acts 5:33-39). When John the Baptist began his public ministry, for instance, the question was immediately asked of him, "Are you the Messiah we are expecting?" (Luke 3:15). Israel was more ready for the Messiah than at any other point in their history.

There is a pattern here that supersedes mere coincidence. Surely God was responsible for this incredible timing. If you believe God could use the timing of these apparently unrelated events to further the work of salvation, then you can also believe God is capable of preparing a place for you in heaven.

I'm certain there are things for which you have given up hope. Like Sarah who waited twenty-five years for the birth of Isaac, then laughed when she was told she would give birth the following year, maybe you too have stopped waiting. What you are hoping for has taken too long to arrive. In the midst of your impatience, remember God doesn't function on your time schedule. God's knowledge of events and what is required to bring about God's plans extends beyond your ability to fathom.

If you believe in a God who timed the birth of the Christchild so precisely, you can also believe in a God who knows the proper timing for you. Maybe you are waiting for someone to get well. Maybe you are waiting for a spouse to attend church with you. Maybe you are looking ahead to the end of apartment living. Maybe you are impatient with your children because they are refusing to learn some of life's major lessons. Whatever you are waiting for, please wait patiently. God's timing is far superior to your own.

The Right People

This census involved the right people, because it involved the Jews. The census affected the entire Jewish nation. The journey so many of them had to make to their ancestral lands forced them to get in touch with their history as a people. They were asked once again to consider the fact that they were the people of God, the people of the covenant made with Abraham, the people from whom the Messiah would come.

The census involved the right people because it affected a carpenter from the village of Nazareth and his young bride who was far advanced in her pregnancy. Other babies were probably born in Bethlehem in those days, perhaps even on the same night Jesus was born. But in order for God's salvation plan to progress it needed to be one family in particular that made the pilgrimage to Bethlehem. And it was their baby in particular who had to be born there. Somehow, God got them involved.

God's ability to involve the right people demonstrates God's ability to be God. Will God's will work any differently in your life than it did back then? The people in your life are there for a reason. God intends to teach you something through them. God intends to teach them something through you. The relationships you enjoy, and those you don't, form a framework in which God shapes you into the divine image. If you ignore this fact and behave as if God does not know what God is doing, then you fail to back up your belief that God involved the right people in the birth of the Christchild.

In the story of Augustus's census, we see God incredibly

working within human plans to meet God's expectations. If God has used the proper authorities at the proper time, and if God involved the proper people to accomplish the work in the coming of Jesus to Bethlehem, surely God can do the same when Jesus returns to set up his eternal kingdom of peace and righteousness.

On that night not so long ago, Mary, Joseph, and the shepherds had no way of fully understanding how God brought about the miraculous event. They only knew God had done and was going to do something wondrous. We have the benefit of looking back and seeing just what God did. This should fill us with a certainty as we consider present circumstances. We can hope in the future because the most unusual circumstances can be used by and for God's purposes.

THE CONSULTATION OF THE MAGI

n the time of King Herod, after Jesus was born in Bethlehem of Judea, wise men from the East came to Jerusalem, asking, "Where is the child who has been born king of the Jews? For we observed his star at its rising, and have come to pay him homage." When King Herod heard this, he was frightened, and all Jerusalem with him; and calling together all the chief priests and scribes of the people, he inquired of them where the Messiah was to be born. They told him, "In Bethlehem of Judea; for so it has been written by the prophet: 'And you, Bethlehem, in the land of Judah, are by no means least among the rulers of Judah; for from you shall come a ruler who is to shepherd my people Israel.'" Then Herod secretly called for the wise men and learned from them the exact time when the star had appeared. Then he sent them to

Bethlehem, saying, "Go and search diligently for the child; and when you have found him, bring me word so that I may also go and pay him homage." **W**hen they had heard the king, they set out; and there, ahead of them, went the star that they had seen at its rising, until it stopped over the place where the child was. **W**hen they saw that the star had stopped, they were overwhelmed with joy. **O**n entering the house, they saw the child with Mary his mother; and they knelt down and paid him homage. **T**hen, opening their treasure chests, they offered him gifts of gold, frankincense, and myrrh. **A**nd having been warned in a dream not to return to Herod, they left for their own country by another road.

Matthew 2:1-12

Within minutes you will arrive at the North Pole by dogsled. Your heart begins pounding. Your breath shortens. Excitement wells within you as you anticipate the end of a months-long adventure.

Your expedition started several years ago when you and your fellow adventurers pored over Arctic maps, plotting how you would accomplish such a feat. Then came the corporate contacts in order to finance the trip. Because you were planning a previously untried route, they came through, staking you with the best equipment on the market. You would lack nothing for your journey. Next came the hard work of preparing the dogs and training yourself to endure the cold.

Finally it was time to leave. A few friends saw you off from a remote point of Canadian wilderness. You shed tears and exchanged fond embraces. Soon the labored breathing of the dogs and sled runners gliding through virgin powder were the only sounds you could hear.

Come to think of it, the excitement you are feeling at the end of the journey is not much different from the excitement on the day you began, only the journey's beginning seems ages ago. One of your friends died in a whiteout. He stepped out to check the dogs and never came back. Two days later you uncovered his frozen corpse where it had fallen—two feet from the safety rope. The rest of you are suffering from frostbite and malnutrition. The food supply ran short when you lost a sled and some dogs to thin ice. You were on the sled when it happened. The others pulled you to safety seconds before the strong ocean currents would have swept you under the ice pack.

In spite of these tragedies you have kept on and are now mere yards from your destination and the plane that will take you home. You raise binoculars to your eyes and scan the horizon. Yes! The plane is there. A few minutes more and you wave to the pilot. You have reached the North Pole.

But now you do a peculiar thing. Instead of standing on this planet's northernmost spot and taking pictures of your three surviving companions, and instead of joking about whichever direction you go from here it will be south, and instead of celebrating the results of your journey, you merely pack up your things and leave. You never bother to stand on the spot you suffered so long to reach. You took a perverse pleasure in the planning and making of the journey, but the arrival had no meaning. That would seem pretty ridiculous, wouldn't it? Why would you make such elaborate plans for a trek to the North Pole and then ignore its existence?

Let's consider the North Pole from another perspective. What if instead of an Arctic explorer you are an Inuit who has always lived in the far North. What if the only world you have known is the vast ice-covered region, complete with polar bears, seals, igloos, and arctic foxes? Would standing on the North Pole have the same meaning for you? Probably not. The North Pole would be just one more snow-covered piece of ice, and any desire to reach it would be significantly reduced.

Living in Fort Wayne was a similar experience. Fort Wayne is my hometown and because this city is so familiar to me, I tend to overlook what might attract a tourist. For instance, I never went to the old fort. I know where it is. I have a good idea what historical purpose the fort serves, but I have never plunked down money for a ticket to go inside. Or it's like New Yorkers who have spent their entire lives under the shadow of the Statue of Liberty, but have yet to take the ferry over to Liberty Island.

But, let's say a history buff from Idaho hears about a great replica of a nineteenth-century fort in a midwestern city and decides to vacation in the region. After weeks of saving and preparations, the family gets in the car and makes the journey to Fort Wayne. Upon arriving, they check into a motel, then head for the downtown library to read about the fort's history. Then they interview people who have been inside the fort. They even take a day to walk around the fort's perimeter. But they never go inside. We would think such a family was rather strange. Why would they expend so much energy for their trip and not pursue their objective?

The wise men were not so foolish. Through a phenomenon unknown to us, they saw a star that led them to conclude that a king worthy of their worship had been born in Judea. So they set out on a long journey from Persia to Jerusalem, the chief city in Judea. When they arrived, they didn't poke around and say, "This must be the place," and "How nice," and then turn around and go home without seeing the Christchild. They aggressively pursued their quest until they knelt at the feet of their infant Lord. These men never lost sight of their objective.

Not so with the chief priest and teachers of the law. Their lives had been so immersed in the Jewish religion that their beliefs had lost meaning for them. Although they knew far more about the birth of the Christchild than the magi, they virtually ignored the event. Following the star to Bethlehem and worshiping the Messiah they had spent so much time studying had no appeal.

Imagine, if you will, what it must have been like during the consultation between Herod and the chief priests and teachers of the law. The arrival of the magi was a newsworthy event. News spread quickly within walled cities and this was no exception, especially because the magi publicly made their desires known. They went through the town asking everyone, "Where is the one who has been born king of the Jews?"

Such a question troubled everyone. It troubled Herod

because although he wasn't born king of the Jews, he had been made king of the Jews by Roman decree thirty-five years earlier. It troubled Herod because he had always been paranoid about anyone who might usurp his throne. He had already killed his wife, mother-in-law, and two sons over these issues.

The magi's question troubled the chief priests and teachers of the law because any sign of a Messiah meant they lost political power. Any hint a Savior had come meant the people would stop following them. It also troubled them because Herod had killed the entire Sanhedrin (the council of Jewish religious leaders) early in his rule and could easily be provoked into doing so again if he thought they had anything to do with this.

The question the magi repeated throughout Jerusalem also troubled the population. Had the Messiah really been born? What would it mean? How would the political leaders respond?

Eventually the magi's question gained them an audience with Herod, but not before he consulted the chief priests and teachers of the law. We should not think these religious leaders worked in unity with one another, nor that they were entirely religious. Their work had become far more political than theological, from at least two contradicting perspectives. The chief priests were largely made up of Sadducees, who were liberal scholars who refused to believe in the afterlife or in heavenly beings. These men were religious only because it was a familiar environment—it was a part of their ethnic heritage. The teachers of the law were mostly conservative Pharisees—strict observers of the most minuscule interpretation of Mosaic Law.

Although these men had few theological beliefs in common, they did have one common cause—power. Together they spoke for the Jewish nation. Together they had access to the ears of Rome, and they were extremely reluctant to give this up.

When Herod put to them the question the magi had been asking, the chief priests and teachers of the law answered with one voice. They dusted off their memories and, as Matthew tells us, gave a rather loose paraphrase of Micah 5, combining two of the verses written there to give Herod his answer. Looking closely at what Micah actually wrote, his prophecy can be summarized as follows:

1. Israel's leadership would remain under the control of other governments until the Messiah came (5:1,3).

2. A new leader of Israel would be born in Bethlehem (5:2,3).

3. This leader would be rooted in the original royal line of Israel (5:2).

4. This leader would reunite the Jewish nation with the strength and majesty of God until God's greatness spread to the ends of the earth (5:4).

If all this was communicated to Herod, it is little wonder he reacted with murderous intent. He spoke in the sweetest tones to the magi, "Go and make a careful search for the child. As soon as you find him, report to me, so that I too may go and worship him." The magi did find the babe and offered gifts of gold, frankincense, and myrrh. The rest of the story is familiar. God warned the magi not to return to Herod, and they made their way home by a different route.

Notice the response of the chief priests and teachers of the law. Do they seek out the Messiah? No. They knew all the prophecies. They were the ones who supplied the necessary information. They were the ones thoroughly immersed in the religion and culture that produced the Messiah, yet they had no interest in finding him. What a horrible example of religious leadership. They were so caught up in the study that they overlooked the meaning.

Are we any different today? Both liberal and conservative religious leaders could be accused of confusing religious beliefs with political agendas. Religious leaders produce a plethora of issue statements, but when was the last time you read one that included a call to come worship the

Christchild? Many who give themselves the name liberal have obviously abandoned the faith. They are so caught up in finding the "historical" Jesus, totally stripped of miraculous legend, that they will never recognize him at his coming. Those who identify themselves as conservative, the keepers of the faith, run into a similar danger. They are so busy discussing the return of Christ, that the actual return would be an interruption.

And what about us? Could it be that in our enthusiasm over being the church we forget the reason the church exists? Could our building of God's kingdom only be a thin disguise for the building of our own? Could our pursuit of the good life lead us to resent the possibility of a second advent? The answers to these questions scare me. As we consider the Christmas event, we must understand that the work of God did not end with the birth of a baby. It continued on to the crucifixion and will not be completed until the second coming of Jesus Christ.

Are we ready for Christ's coming, or are we like the chief priests and teachers of the law, immersed in the information but totally indifferent to the meaning? Alexander MacLaren has written, "The most impenetrable armor against the gospel is the familiar and lifelong knowledge of the gospel" (*Expositions of Holy Scripture: Matthew,* Grand Rapids: Eerdmans, 1938, p. 24).

We must learn to look at the Christ event from first to second advent with the worshipful eyes of the magi. Let us start our journey over again and begin looking for our Lord. And, as an Arctic explorer would do upon reaching the North Pole, may we celebrate the arrival.

THE SLAUGHTER OF THE INNOCENTS

ow after they had left, an angel of the Lord appeared to Joseph in a dream and said, "Get up, take the child and his mother, and flee to Egypt, and remain there until I tell you; for Herod is about to search for the child, to destroy him." Then Joseph got up, took the child and his mother by night, and went to Egypt, and remained there until the death of Herod. This was to fulfill what had been spoken by the Lord through the prophet, "Out of Egypt I have called my son." When Herod saw that he had been tricked by the wise men, he was infuriated, and he sent and killed all the children in and around Bethlehem who were two years old or under, according to the time that he had learned from the wise men. Then was fulfilled what had been spoken through the prophet Jeremiah: "A voice was heard in Ramah, wailing and loud lamentation,

Rachel weeping for her children; she refused to be consoled, because they are no more." When Herod died, an angel of the Lord suddenly appeared in a dream to Joseph in Egypt and said, "Get up, take the child and his mother, and go to the land of Israel, for those who were seeking the child's life are dead." Then Joseph got up, took the child and his mother, and went to the land of Israel.

Matthew 2:13-21

Nearly two thousand years ago a soothsayer told the Roman Senate that a king was to be born that year. Legend said this king would be powerful enough to overthrow the most oppressive regime. Rumors flew fast. Some thought the Senate was considering ordering the exposure of every newborn child. But as time passed, the legend was dismissed and no more attention was given to the matter.

The Bible adds more detail to the story. The child-king was the baby Jesus. King Herod was the ruler who ordered the murder of the innocents. The parents forewarned by God and who made their escape by night were Joseph and Mary. The place where this occurred was the town of Bethlehem. The mothers who lost their children were descendants of Rachel.

This is a tragedy-filled story—a tragedy similar to events we read about in the paper each day, but seldom experience personally. Suffering and injustice do not always escape us. We recognize its icy touch, yet we who live in North America are in the shallows compared to the depth of suffering for major portions of this planet.

As we look closely at the horrible events of this drama, we will discover that they do not lessen the impact of the advent. In fact, God uses them to accomplish his purpose. Just as it didn't lessen the impact of the advent, whatever suffering, tragedy, or injustice I experience will not lessen the impact of God's work in me.

Herod's father, Antipater, had been an old crony of Julius Caesar and Caesar Augustus, helping them to conquer territories that later became the Roman Empire. Such access to the highest halls of power brought opportunities to Antipater's Edomite family. His son, Herod, received a governorship in Palestine as a young man, and later was named tetrarch over the region. Palestine was unstable at this time, however, and a Parthian invasion forced him to flee to Rome. While in Rome, Herod was appointed king over Judea, and with Roman forces backing him, he retook Jerusalem and ascended the throne. He immediately put the members of the Sanhedrin to death and began a reign mixed with benevolence and terror.

It was a custom for rulers, even oppressive ones, to serve as benefactors for their subjects—at personal expense. Herod was no exception. He fashioned gardens, pools, and other public places of leisure. He built fortresses, the most famous of which is Masada. He even restored the temple in Jerusalem. At the same time, however, he put to death anyone who threatened his rule, including a number of family members. Even on his deathbed he called the nobility to his bedside so they could be murdered at his passing. He did this so Israel would mourn, not rejoice, at his demise. Hearing the character of Herod's rule led Augustus to say, "It is better to be Herod's pig than his son." Since the statement was made in Greek, it carried a special irony. The words "pig" and "son" in Greek are only one letter different in spelling.

By the time of Christ's birth Herod was an old man. One of his surviving sons would soon succeed him. He was probably already fatally ill when the magi arrived asking where the newborn king could be found, but it did not stop him from making another attempt to preserve his throne. Originally he hoped to fool the magi into revealing the location of the Christchild. Then, under the pretense of going to worship this babe himself, he would have him killed. But with God's help the magi outwitted him.

Herod had always been a careful man. Familiar with the push and pull of political intrigue, he liked to keep his options open. So what if the magi had fooled him? He would teach them how to play tricks. The magi had revealed the time of the star's arrival. It only took a little calculation to estimate the length of their travel from Persia to Palestine. The chief priests and teachers of the law had told him which town would host the birth of the Messiah. Since no one would identify the Christchild for him, why not kill all the children two years and under in Bethlehem and the surrounding countryside? Such an effort was sure to eliminate the Christchild as well. The reign of Herod's family would be guaranteed for another generation.

God intervened once again. In a dream God informed Joseph of Herod's intent and instructed him to flee with Mary and the baby to Egypt and remain there until told otherwise.

The escape ensured the preservation of the Christchild; the plan of God would continue.

The Flight of Refugees

Fleeing to Egypt meant traveling—by foot and in fear—a minimum of seventy-five miles. It was probably one hundred miles more to any Jewish community of significance. Joseph, Mary, and the baby had become refugees. No one wishes to be torn from the familiar and thrust into a foreign environment. Doing so brings a feeling of helplessness unparalleled in human experience. Yet God used this horrible event to further identify the Christchild as the promised one of Israel.

Matthew, the apostle who penned this story for us, tosses in a statement God made through the prophet Hosea: "Out of Egypt I called my son" (11:1). When we study the context of Hosea's writing, we can quickly see that the passage is referring to Israel as the rebellious son whom God brought up from Egypt. There is no indication Hosea was speaking about the Messiah at all. Yet, because Jesus would spend time in Egyptian exile he would share in the history of Israel. This would give him further right to represent Israel as Messiah and king—a theme Matthew seems to take special pains to present. God used the horrible event of becoming a refugee to further validate the fact that this baby was truly the Messiah.

Today, the world is home to a considerable number of refugees, many of them Christians. Some flee because of political oppression. Others flee from war. Still others flee because of natural events, like drought-induced famine. Each refugee has seen the familiar environment give way and become an unknown place, yet, many of them turn to this story of Christ's refugee status and find hope for their situation. Yvonne Dilling, a Central American church worker in the mid-1980s, wrote about the faith of Salvadoran refugees who lived in Honduran refugee camps:

> The Salvadoran people here are deeply religious and faithful. One of the earliest things they requested when we built the camp was a tent they could turn into a chapel by putting in a simple cross and some benches. Although far too small to hold all the people, it would be a sacred place where they could go on their own to pray and recite their rosaries.
>
> (Yvonne Dilling, *In Search of Refuge,* Scottdale: Herald Press, 1984, p.76)

If Salvadoran people forced to flee their war-torn homeland and take nothing with them can retain their faith in a God who works on their behalf, why can't we do the same?

The Murder of Babies

Herod carried out his scheme by ordering his soldiers to go door-to-door in Bethlehem and the surrounding areas and execute male children under two years of age. Biblical scholars estimate as many as sixty babies lost their lives—not large on the scale of historical massacres, but no small tragedy either. Some of these boys would have been newly born, perhaps still covered with their mother's fluids. Some may have been sucking down mother's milk for the first time. Others would have been recently circumcised, revealing covenanted flesh when the soldiers tore away their cloths to reveal their sex. A few babies would have been teething. Some would have begun crawling or walking. Still others would have just begun to say comprehendible words. Now they were gone.

Thinking about such an event raises many difficult questions, questions we are reluctant to ask. How could God allow it? How could God stand by and let Herod live while he carried out his wickedness? If this Christchild was to represent peace on earth, why is his birth surrounded by such destruction? Why does the Christchild get to live, while so many others died?

I have no answers to these questions. No one short of God could ever fully answer them. However, we do know Jesus said he didn't come to bring peace but a sword (Matthew 10:34). We do know he said that following him would mean persecution and even death (Matthew 24:9). We also know various forces have competed throughout history for the authority only Jesus Christ holds. When evil powers struggle to overcome what is good, innocent people die. This is how it always has been and any accounting we demand of God will not change the suffering that innocents experience. So we have a choice. We can reject God and ultimately believe life has no meaning, or we can embrace the story of the Christchild—a story that reveals a God capable of working in spite of horrible events.

Everyday experience is full of innocent victims of false arrest and vindictive legal suits, of people maimed by drunk drivers, of babies addicted to the drugs their mothers consumed while pregnant, of rape, incest, burglary, and so on. How will we respond? With despair? Anger? Or with a renewed hope that a God who worked within horrible events to ensure the salvation of the human race is doing so now as God works within us?

The Mourning of Mothers

Not only has a family been forced to flee, and not only have children lost their lives, but their mothers were forced to witness the slaughter. Now, these mothers began their lament.

Matthew again quotes an Old Testament prophet, this time Jeremiah: "A voice is heard in Ramah, lamentation and bitter weeping. Rachel is weeping for her children; she refuses to be comforted for her children, because they are no more" (31:15). The context of this image when God spoke through Jeremiah was the captivity of Israel. As Israel travels from the homeland to the place of captivity, the sound of weeping and mourning rises from Rachel's grave. Rachel, the wife of the patriarch Jacob, was viewed as the mother of Israel. Her weeping symbolized the grief felt at the loss of her children's nationality.

Matthew sees in this a parallel to the experience of Bethlehem's mothers. More of Rachel's children had been murdered. Her daughters now took up her cry of grief as their own. Matthew's use of this prophetic image is especially poignant because Rachel's grave was near Bethlehem, the place these horrible events occurred.

Have you ever grieved so deeply that your body heaved from sorrow? If so, the indelible impression this leaves gives you insight into the mourning of Bethlehem's mothers. Some would have been mothers for the first time, perhaps just days or even hours earlier. Others would have waited a long time to give birth to a son, a special occasion to a Jew because it meant the family's claim to an inheritance in Israel continued for another generation. Some mothers would have been nursing their children or cradling them to sleep after waking during the night. Other mothers would have been exasperated with their child, no more finished yelling at their child to be quiet than the soldiers burst into the room. Now there would be no more nursing, no more nuzzling the softness of their child, no opportunity to express love any longer.

Yet, in the midst of their grief, we find hope. Just as these children lost their lives and their mothers had to grieve over them, the Christchild would also eventually be slain and grief would be brought to his mother. And in that death would be salvation.

Is there a grief you carry? Is there a sorrow in your life that seems to know no end? Surely this grief is no greater than the grief of Bethlehem's mothers, or the grief Mary would feel at the crucifixion of her son. Yet, as the Gospel story unfolds we see women assisting Jesus in his ministry. After his ascension into heaven we see these women, including his mother, assisting in the establishment of the church. In the midst of their suffering they held on to the hope that a loving God was in charge. Can you do the same in the midst of your pain?

Consider the horrible events surrounding the Christmas story. They cannot lessen the impact of the advent. Realizing this helps me believe that God continues the same work today—in my life and in the world in which I live.

About the Author

Mark Vincent is minister of youth for the Indiana-Michigan Mennonite Conference, along with his wife, Lorie. They also direct the adult program for Camp Amigo, located near Sturgis, Michigan. Their work focuses on the creation of networking programs for improved congregational life.

A native of Fort Wayne, Indiana, Mark returned there in 1983 to serve as youth pastor and later as lead pastor at First Mennonite Church. He and his family moved to Michigan in 1992.

Mark has been chair of the Justice, Peace, and Service Commission of the Indiana-Michigan Mennonite Conference and a member of the Alumni Advisory Board to Taylor University—Fort Wayne. He was named to Who's Who in Religion in 1992.

Mark and Lorie have two children, Autumn and Zachary.